STORMS AND ANCHOR

Reflections on mortality, disillusionment and succour

Dedication

In memory of Chinonso,

Whose exit remains a fresh slit on the palm,

That hurts with every washing of hands.

Acknowledgements

Profound thanks to the following:

Christian Ovbokhan Otabor, the glowing coal that rekindles a cold fireplace.

Ele Chimezie Egwu,for always blowing the flute when the legs become too heavy for the dance.

Henry Amaefule, Joel Ukaegbu, James Okorukwu, Emeka Egeonu and Ezeudo Maduka for lending a hand when the trail became slippery.

Adrian and Andrea,allies both in distress and delight.

And Bethel Ugwuagbo,who illuminates my path when it is dark.

Preface

Storms and Anchor is an emotional outburst expressed in poetic form reflecting on human mortality, unfulfilled expectations, the ensuing despair and a strong conviction that solace is extant. Heartfelt feelings and longings are painted in words with strong African hue where proverbs are dexterously used to beautify and echo the emotions expressed in each poem.

The poems take one on a journey of the realities of existence and the innate desire for succour.

Table of Contents

Title Page

Dedication

Acknowledgements

Preface

Contents

SECTION 3-SUBTERFUGE

SECTION 4-REALITIES

SECTION ONE- MORTALITY

Mortality

When my maiden cry pierced the silence of dawn,
Songs bubbled like a spring.
The sands of time wooed my feet
And clamoured for their royal prints.
My footprint the world indeed saw,
For the buffetings of fate, I bore well,
From cruel whips I did not shudder,
Till dark clouds gathered
And the shroud became king.
Now the faithful red mound
Is the custodian of my nothingness.

My History

Where wild orchids in perfect bloom
Dwelt among meadows in verdant plume
Where gazelles basked in the rising sun
There I first saw the sun.
The hills all radiant and green
(And the world too was green)
Welcomed me with a warm embrace
And caressed my ruddy face.
The rain fell for the sky was gray,
This idyll was washed away
Orchids, meadows, all were gone-
Smothered by winds that maim and scorn.
I parried these blows of fate
Stinging, furious and full of hate
Till my hands for want of rest
Bade farewell and went to rest.

This Journey We All Make

This journey we all make
Through this winding path
Scorched by the sun's anger.
It scalds our bare feet
Already torn by thorns.
The rains make it slippery,
We fall and bruise our knees.
Like wool drifting in the wind,
We are tossed about
Until we reach the great sea
Where the dying flames of our torch
Are finally extinguished.
While the lonely buds
Manured by our eternal silence
Become the memorials
Of this solemn journey.

We Shall Still See at Dawn

When the sun sets on me
While my work is still not done
And my songs flee from me
When it is not yet dawn,
You may cry but let me be
For we shall still see at dawn.
Even though you search for my laughter
From the shadows of our past
Or long for words I did utter
Before death's bugle blast,
You may cry but let me be
For we shall still see at dawn.

A Short Span

Dawn comes with a song
That is soon sung.
Then arrives the solemnness of nightfall
And the call that awaits all.
Where the sorrowful notes of the flute
Blend with the owl's hoot,
As mourners await their turn
To be mourned in return.

SECTION TWO-TEARS

Tears

The moon was full.
The moon was bright.
Her mirth infected me.
The valleys echoed my laughter.

Rainclouds became envious.
The moon was swallowed.
My song went cold.

Then my smoldering incense reached the clouds.
The rain was appeased.
I looked out for the moon-
The friendly full moon.
But a crescent is all I see.
Her feeble brilliance
Makes just a silhouette
Of my sunny days.

Why?

When I'm pierced by darts of fate
And my eyes swim in tears
My plea for solace is scorned and strangled
I face the sky and ask why.
I tread on paths slippery and winding,
I fall and my shin is bloodied
And as thorns hurry to dress my wounds
I face the sky and ask why.
Sorrow drips from my soul
While succor curls in the womb
And with eyes that swim in tears
I face the sky and ask why.

In the Crucible

Like the sting of warring wasps
Despair gnaws at my heart
As I recall my travails
In the confines of this crucible.

I was once clad in imperial garments,
The fragrance of roses caressed my nostrils
And the songs of birds soothed my ears.
But the sun suddenly went black,
And darkness shredded my clothes.
I lost the table on which I dined
And started eating on the floor.

My sweat watered a young tree
From the nursery to the field,
But amid its season of laughter,
It succumbed to the savage storm.

I battled for light in the lion's den.
I was bruised and lost a limb.
But at last I got the flame,
Which flickered and died on my doorstep.

When shall my silent clamours
Appease the heat of this crucible?
I am just striking the wind,
And my prayers are a message to the birds.

Should I extinguish the smoldering faggot
That has scorned illumination,
Then take a mouthful of hemlock wine
And sink into eternal oblivion?

But I hear a silent song,
From the bowels of hope.
It has the chorus of happy birds
That herald days sunny and bright.

Prayer of the Broken-Hearted

Father, where are you?
Please give ear to my plea.
Those I started the race with have gone far,
And I am left far behind.
For my legs have grown feeble,
Too feeble to carry my weight,
That I fall with each stride.
Going forward is a great ordeal,
Going backward a stigma of cowardice.
Did I desecrate your consecrated ground?
Did I cause the treachery of man?
Or are my teeth set on edge
Because of unripe fruit eaten by others?
My heart is always bleeding
From pangs of sorrow and pain.
My eyelids are heavy
From an ocean of tears.
Each night, ghosts torment me
In the day, phantoms ridicule me.
When the wind blows,
Needles caress my skin.
When the birds sing,
It is dirges I hear.
I wanted to find succor
By taking the course of Judas
When he realized his greed for silver
Had caused the shedding of sinless blood

But I abhor the ignominy of self annihilation.
Please, the Benevolent One,
Deliver me from this abyss of despair
For in my own mortal imagination
I have done no wrong.
But if You say I am not guiltless,
Forgive and lift me up.

Fortitude

At the crossroads,
Far from the shade of the palm
Bereft of its fronds,
The sun smacked my back
With the fury of a vengeful scorpion.
I shut my eyes to its blinding rays.
Then I saw its flaming tentacles
Swipe my aching heart
And clothe it with a skin
To bear fiercer buffetings of fate.

Daybreak

(To Armstrong)

Remember those days when mists of uncertainty
Shrouded our timid hearts.
We never left the hearthstead,
The fire of which burned from our silent prayers
And our hopes blossomed into a fortress
That brimmed with ripples of success.
Remember the tears we shed together,
Tears that soaked the soil
For our footprints to be visible.
The thunder barked in fury,
Who did not rear with foreboding?
But we did not cower
Because hope had a home in our hearts.
It stood like a citadel held by loyal rocks.
Malevolent winds snarling with spite
And bloated with hate,
We kicked with sturdy feet
That sparkled with crystals of confidence.

But the storms have invaded our yearnings.
Now our path has become slippery
From the mire of battered expectations.
Brutal hands of fate have uprooted our dreams
Leaving them on the roadside to wither.
Our hope has become a crushed reed
Being trampled to a sad death.

Our hearts have grown cold-
Their mirth stolen by the sobbing moon
Clad in garbs of mourning.

But I see beyond this bleakness
A day coming with kerchiefs of comfort
To clean our tears.
I see that day when our withering dreams
Shall drink life to the full
And blossom like daffodils drenched in dew.
The day shall break
When our tearful hearts
Shall have the taste of happy songs.
The moon shall discard her sackcloth
For flowing gowns of glee
And sing a joyful chorus.
That day shall break!

Sunken Joy

Like leaves scorched by the sun
The heart withers,
Her songs grow cold,
Her joys get sunk.

Hopes that blossomed into a fortress
Have been battered by tempests of change,
Hopes that scorned incertitude
Trembled, cracked and were squashed.
But patience, cure of crumbled hopes
Lies lifeless in ruins of shattered dreams
And the mute nagging of stillborn expectations
Quenches the fire in the heart.
Then the heart withers,
Her songs grow cold,
Her joys get sunk.

Tale of Woes

Shall the stars ever smile on me
Or the sun dry my tears?
I shiver in the cold of my fears
As this rain falls on me.

I arrived without fanfare.
I did not defile the air.
Yet I hurt and bleed in dread
From arrows of hurt and dread.

Thistles and thorns bask in my fields,
They scoff at my weeping yields
While termites and locusts sharpen their teeth
And prepare a feast for their kith.

In my travails I am alone,
The weight of my tears crushes my bone.
I grovel on the feet of succor
To be admitted through her door.

Soon shall my relief arrive
In showers of joyous rest.
My joys and laughter shall thrive
In the luxury of a happy harvest.

Suicide Note

The sun saw me and hid his face,
The stars frowned on hearing my voice,
The birds rained curses from mid heavens,
The thunder stuttered in bitter protest,
The sea became restive in her tantrum,
The clouds cried with no consolation.
Why?
Probably I alighted on the wrong stop.
So I will continue my journey
To where the sun shall embrace me,
To where the stars are full of smiles,
To where the birds sing praises,
To where the thunder shall demolish my woes,
To where the sea shall rinse my sweat,
And the clouds clothe me in royal raiment.
There I shall pitch my tent
With my torch to light darkened paths.

But the sound of reason tells me
That a bit of being
Is better than oblivion.

The Sorrow in My Heart is Great.

When the swift stumble in a race
And a warrior loses a battle,
The indolent eats better than a king,
And sneers at hard work,
The sorrow in my heart is great.

When the dog has a feast of dung,
And his teeth glow and sparkle,
But the goat's teeth become rotten
After eating mere fodder,
The sorrow in my heart is great.

When a foal is watered and fed
Until she becomes a mare,
Then gets saddled for a ride
Only to break her owner's backbone,
The sorrow in my heart is great.

When a tree smiles in the dew,
Its bark humming a pleasant tune,
But the whirlwind blows,
And the tree is uprooted,
The sorrow in my heart is great.

When the tortoise outruns the hare
And makes jest of the antelope's stride,
The deer laughs in derision,

At the lameness of the leopard,
The sorrow in my heart is great.

There remains one more thing,
(In fact, the father of them all),
That torments my weary soul,
With sorrow that is great:
EXPECTATION POSTPONED!

Snapped Sword

"How are the mighty ones fallen
And the weapons of war perished!".
Tears of punctured hearts
Have filled a dozen baskets
And the wailing of sealed lips
Still tingles the ears.

The fragrance of hateless love
For the mound that held your father's bones
Was so strong in your nostrils
That you left your half-built hut
With swords sharpened by your bravery
To attack invading hyenas.

The Earth was drunk with fear,
The stallion became a lamb,
Warriors cowered like a beaten dog,
When you muffled the angry peal of the thunder.
The elusive beast
That mocked the skill of hunters
You picked from his concealed corner
And your kinsmen robed you with laurels.

Today the horns overwhelm us with plaintive
notes-
The giant tree has fallen!
The clogged wheels of the chariot

Lie desolate on the mountain.
The sword has been snapped in two
And the shield devoured by rust.
For the lion has given one last roar
And lies lifeless on garlands of valour.
"How have the mighty ones fallen
And the weapons of war perished!"

At Last!

At last it has arrived,
The firefly that illuminates the darkness
Of this cold harmattan night.

My torch was doused
By brutal rain of woes.
I washed my hands clean
Only to crack palm kernel for the hens.
Despair clung like a wet clothe
To my soul sunk in sorrow.
But in my quest for warmth,
A rat licked my face.

Now at last it has arrived,
The blinking light of the firefly,
To help me grope my way
To the end of this slippery path
That ushers in the warmth
That may dry the tears on my face.

SECTION THREE -SUBTERFUGE

Mirage

Mounting the podium, oaths are taken.
Sleeping hopes are roused
By honeyed chants of lips
Kissing the scepter.

Our hands are spread wide
In jubilant expectation of rain
To cool our fevers.

But alas! Our hands have become heavy
Waiting for lost rains
In the forked tongue of a serpent.
Now a string of broken promises
Send our roused hopes
Back to a deep slumber.

Affairs of the State

I came across a senator today.
His forehead gleams from luxury,
And cheeks swollen from lavish banquets.
"Dear Sir", I called with a bow,
"How's the affairs of the state?"
"My most honoured comrade", he replied,
"Affairs of the state give me sleepless nights.
I opened a new scroll today,
And the 'ayes' had their way.
Tomorrow perhaps, the pauper will have a feast.
I am hurrying home for a bite,
Affairs of the state deprive us of victuals"
He swaggered to his car,
Pretense trailed his back.
He belched and murmured:
"The House was aglow with meat and wine,
Now I cannot sleep this night
With this abundance of food and drink.
Affairs of the state do give me sleepless nights!"

Defiled

In your bosom we are cradled,
Our thirst is assuaged.
You clothe us in white garbs
That assure us of celestial banquets.
In your bosom the chameleon sings,
He whispers words of endearment,
As he coaxes you to the tables
Where you cast lots in his favour
And crown him with wreaths of power.

Oh! Mender of my soul,
You've been defiled by the chameleon,
Whose rhetorics rouse our somnolent hopes
That soon sink into slumber
While your protégés engage in brawls
Induced by the aroma of power.

Silent Plea

My naked palms face the heavens
Like knees bent in wordless entreaty
Before the shrine of a benevolent god.
Would their wordless appeal
Prick the heart of the Valiant One
Whose footprints grace unexplored paths?
He will send rivers of nemesis
To drown the valorous and brave
Who glean the fields of the fatherless
With sickles of oppression.

Unshackled!

Yesterday,
I was shrouded in shadows of gloom
In the belly of this fortress of hate
Where rats robed in malice
Gnawed at my heart bloated with pus.
The echoes of mirth from my kith and kin
Had been drowned by the ululations
Of lips silenced by a horde of scorpions.
Clang! The macabre chuckle of the hangman
Had announced a hearty breakfast of blood
Gushing with sad melancholy
To the tables of red-eyed vultures...

I am the Galileo among my brethren,
my creed is like the sun at noon-
never blurred by dark clouds
but smothers the incense of deceit
burned by envoys of discord.
'His gospel is a garrote to our game', they said.
'cut the stem for the leaves to wither'.
Then a last look (it seemed) at my unploughed
farm
And the gates closed behind me.

Today,
The blazing sun has pierced the darkness of
gloom!

And now I am flying over these walls of misery.
I shall pass seven seas and seven forests
Where I shall smear my kith and kin
With the fragrant oil of truth.
We shall wage war on the vultures.
We shall drive them into the desert
To sink with the setting sun.
Then we shall embrace our wives,
And run into the arms of our friends
Amid the booming of cannons
Announcing the birth of freedom.

Nightfall at Noon

Under the shade of the Iroko tree
That towered above my father's hut,
There we were playing hide-and-seek
Oblivious of the mid-day heat.
A cock boasting behind the brush,
A goat scolding her errant kids,
The squabble of naked children,
Mingled with the flute and gong.

But suddenly, the crack of thunder!
Its command curdled our blood.
"Pack and Quit! All of you!",
The volcano roared spilling its lava.
Amid a riot of emotions, we ran,
The rat and the lizard fought for right of way,
Hot tears scalded our cheeks
At the shattered serenity of our home.
Falling walls and burning bans
Echoed the peremptory command,
And quit we must
But to pack was impossible.

The journey was a bumpy one.
On the winding way to shelter
That existed in the realms of our faith,
We stooped from spree to squalor,
We dwelt with disease and death,

And languished in laments and languor.
The journey was a bumpy one,
All because a rising sun
Was not given the chance
To spread its rays abroad.

Certitude

From the safety of my unsafe hut
I see justice fluttering on broken wings,
Battered by tempests of tyranny.
Smoking chimneys of smothered truths
Dress the sun in mourning clothes
And the lifeless carcass of freedom
Rots on the rubbish heap.
But a bell tolls unceasingly in my heart
Like the glorious chants of Cherubs.
Its rhythm is the running of chariots
Ushering days that sparkle with liberty.

Entreaty

Amid the hisses and rattles
Of shameless emissaries of rift,
The nagging voice of virtue proclaims:
"Quench this conflagration!
Why set the house ablaze
To smite a thieving rat?
For when dogs pull down their shelter
Over a piece of dry bone,
They make themselves victim
Of the midnight downpour"

Let the flame of peace
Light up our hearts darkened by hate.
Let the sounds from drums of peace
Drown the hissing of our hate.
The thick wall of distrust
Which had blurred the light of brotherliness
Will be razed by our mutual smiles.
Then our sons shall learn
To eat from the same pot.

Boomerang

Your sword drips with blood,
The bitter blood of unknown heroes
Who refuse to swallow the excreta
Gushing from your putrid throne of tyranny.

How many severed heads are in your basket?
Their mute protests pierce the clouds.
We offered you our guileless sweat
And hoped for soft showers
To cool our fevered bodies.
But you kicked us in the face
Leaving us with nasal hemorrhage.

Now prepare to dance to the song
From the drumbeats of justice.
Be ready to entertain the lizards
That visit your ant-infested faggots.
Our eyes were wide open
When you reached the top of the Iroko.
Our eyes shall remain open
When you fall and burst your belly.

Dead Days

Those days are dead
When swarthy skins bled
From the cruel whips of strangers.
When the sweat of black heroes
Nourished unknown soils.
When liberty curled in the womb,
And the seed of freedom
Was burnt in the barrel of firearms.
Those were the days when cudgels of scorn
Maimed the beauty of Nubian root.
But the chrysalis crawled out of its cocoon
And vexed by the whimpers of warriors
Spewed restive waters
That drowned the bitter days.

Wishes

I am the lamenting voice,
Muffled by the revelries of the marauding beast
Who reaps the crops of my brothers
Crippled by rabid dogs that feast on cruelty.
I shout my voice hoarse
Coaxing the winds of liberty
To blow the breath of life
Into the languid body of freedom.
I implore the forests and the seas
To echo the sounds of jubilee.
Let them beat hard on drums of freedom
For wicked walls of cruelty to crumble
And floods of shackled limbs
To embrace the bosom of liberty.

SECTION FOUR-REALITIES

Restive Tongues

Restive tongues with endless chatter
Wallow in puddles of spiteful tales.
They wink with eyes that see only darkness,
Their feet and fingers loudly announce
The sour stench of unbridled malice.

A cluster of hollow heads
Bound together by withered tendrils
Take furtive glances at nothing
And nod like the Agama
In tacit agreement with twisted truths
Woven into a tapestry of defamation
That wipe the glister off faithful faces
And hurl the virtuous into a mire.

They breathe lies from their nostrils
And raze the neighborhood with scorching flames
That heap heavy sorrow on dainty hearts.

Façade

In showers of endless gaiety
Dripping comfort and suavity
My garments sparkling with luxury
Hide the agony of my misery.

"Fate has been good to you,
You are rich and seldom sad"
Oh! How I pray for these two-
To be rich and seldom sad.

Impostors

Fatty banquets are all they know,
They hail me, they make me king.
My faithful pockets that never say no
Beat the drum as they sing.

The wind is howling with hate!
It grabs me in its treacherous tail!
"Comrades! A rope decides my fate!"
But all I grab is a gecko's tail.

When Fury Reigns

When fury reigns in glory,
Civility is crucified,
Thinking is tossed unto thorns
And folly sneers at virtue...

Boiling blood has sipped
The sobering syrup of time
And conscience whips the mind
With the flagella of reason.
Then bliss becomes elusive-
Smothered by the cicatrix
Of a transient folly.

Transient Illusions

When somnolence seals my eyes
And sobriety in lifelessness lies,
My soul sails into serenity,
Away from the harsh peals of reality.
The lullabies of Eden I hear,
I feel not the stings of fear,
Undisturbed I roam in perfection
Till wakefulness steals my illusion.

Time

Always on the move,
She never ceases to prove
A detour is impossible
As God is infallible.
No hill is as old,
No warrior is as bold,
The past is her possession,
The future is her motion.
She speaks with a reechoing chime.
She is TIME!

Lip Service

The sun blazed like a hearth
Upon the helpless earth
As I strutted from the stream,
My calabash filled to the brim.
I saw him lose his footing,
He fell and hurt his shin
But he fixed his gaze on me,
Cleared his throat and spoke to me:
"Please, a mouthful brother
To quench this raging thirst,
I am sorry this is a bother
But give me a mouthful first"
"Your timing is wrong, brother
Because I am late to church.
Please endure your thirst
Till I return from the church".

In the church I sang
Until my voice grew hoarse,
I knelt in the pew and prayed
For the good of all my neighbours.

I opened my eyes
And saw the funeral procession.
"A mouthful would have saved him",
I heard the mourners say.
"May his soul rest in peace",
I replied and wept.

Nostalgia

When the snow falls,
Stabbing my heart with cold,
I long for my mother's hearth
That shielded us from the harmattan.
I perceive the aroma of burning logs
And the golden flame that cooked our food,
I inhale the redolence
Of clay pots sitting on the fire.
I feel the smoothness of cold ash
On our soles and hairless skin,
I hear my mother calling us
For a bath warm and soothing.

When night comes with a labyrinth of bulbs
And the hubbub of casinos,
I remember my humble home
Where night and day respect their boundaries.
I see the moon smiling from above,
Her radiant face illuminating the village square,
Where we listened to the exploits of the wise tortoise
From the croaking voice of my grandmother.

When I am reminded that I am a stranger,
I remember my father's vast kingdom.
An aura of respect surround me
As I walk through the bush path
With the wild paying homage to me.

When shall I shed this coat of fur
For the warmth of mother's hearth?
When shall I hear from my hut
The heartbeat of an undiluted night?
When shall I water the mound
Where my afterbirth was interred?
When shall I roast cocoyam
On the smoldering ash of the oil bean wood

How I long to cross this ocean
To chew a lobe of my father's kolanut.

Downpour

The million drops of falling rain
drumming placidly on the roofs
sing a lullaby of unspoken words
that soothes the soul with somnolence.

The earth drips with slimy wetness
like a pig wallowing in a puddle,
The ponds are drunk to saturation,
their frothing vomit run rapidly
into rivers that bristle with ripples.
The clouds wear a gloomy mask
that hides the sun's smiles,
and the grumbling of the thunder
leaves the trees limp and doleful.

In the bosom of a hundred huts,
the flickering of golden flames,
breathes life to slumbering.
While the heart beats to the rhythm
of the million drops of falling rain,
drumming placidly on the roofs,
singing a lullaby of unspoken words
that soothes the soul with somnolence.

To the Bride and Groom

Now that your hearts have finally met,
These reminders do not forget:
Live everyday with love as a guide,
Always cherish your groom and your bride.
Share with yourselves the hilarious things,
And the melodies of when your heart sings.
Remember to make God a third cord,
At all times feeding from His word.
Do not let the sun set while you're angry,
To make peace you should always hurry.
Be a pillar for each other to lean on,
In times of both distress and fun.
Open your ears to listen well
And set your tongue to speak what is well.
Make your mate your best friend,
Your hearts and hands always ready to lend.
From this day on never be apart,
Wherever you are, your spouse remains your part.
And when time has passed and two of you age,
When your book nears the final page,
You will not see the wrinkles nor the gray,
But the splendor of each passing day.

Lesson

See his face shriveled by grief.
He sags under the weight of vileness
That has blossomed into burdens of misery.
His voice once the terrifying thunder
That sent men cowering in fear
Plead unceasingly for assuaging water.
But the silent howls of guiltless blood
Poured on the streets at his orders
Muffle his pleas and sing:
"The storms that strangle your sleep
Are your daily sins that evaporate
To form clouds of vengeful hailstones
That pelt down furiously
And pierce you with a million darts"

Dialogue

"Great Sculptor
In your presence I am
With my forehead
Touching the ground.
I am here
With entreaties
You alone can bear".
"Pour them at my feet.
But do not forget
It's ripe corns only
That I hang on my eaves".
"My legs, Great Sculptor,
They are sturdy.
But also bandy they are.
It is my wish
You touch them
And make them comely
Like a pretty damsel's".
"Ask from your neighbour
Whose buttocks
Calloused by friction
Take him without grudging
To wherever he goes"
"My eyes, Great Sculptor
Cannot see through the wall.
What if, Great Sculptor
You create them anew?

Make the lashes fluffy
Like newly hatched chicks"
"See that man
Behind the walking stick.
Darkness and pitch darkness
Are all he sees.
Then ask the serpent
Where he got his fluffy eyelashes"
"Now about my voice,
Good in oratory only.
Would you Great Sculptor
Make it melodious too?
Sweeter than the nightingale's"
"Look!
Behind your proud back.
Tell me what you see"
"A man gesticulating
With his hands and head.
He cannot utter
Even a single word
For his vocal chords, no doubt
Can only produce silence"
"You answered well.
When a dog thinks
He does not run fast
Let him watch the snail
And the crippled tortoise
Compete in a race"
"But my Lord,

Will it be wrong
If you give me wings?
I will perch on a peak.
I will see those
Who defile the air
And fracture their arms,
Then gently hurl
A handful of dew
On withering crops"
"The pompous bush rat
Wanting to be seen by all
Stood on an anthill
And was devoured
By a colony of termites.
Craning your neck
To see the crown
Of the giraffe's head
Will only break your neck.
So let the water
Your mouth can hold
Quench your thirst."
"Finally my Lord
Answer me this:
Why does a leper
Want an embrace
If you allow him
A handshake?"
"You are the child
Stroking a bird's beak

And still asks the father,
"From where does a bird eat?".
Answer your own question
For you are much worse
Than a leper.
Why should a monkey ask
Why the squirrel
Disturbs the tree
When at play?"
"Forgive me Lord.
I will let the water
My mouth can hold
Quench my thirst".

Printed in Great Britain
by Amazon

87013571R00041